SECRET NEIGHBORS

OTHER BOOKS BY MARY ADRIAN

Hastings House

NATURE MYSTERIES

THE GHOST TOWN MYSTERY

THE LIGHTSHIP MYSTERY

THE KITE MYSTERY

THE INDIAN HORSE MYSTERY

THE MYSTERY OF THE DINOSAUR BONES

THE SKIN DIVING MYSTERY

THE MYSTERY OF THE NIGHT EXPLORERS

THE RARE STAMP MYSTERY

THE FOX HOLLOW MYSTERY

THE URANIUM MYSTERY

THE PRESERVE OUR WILDLIFE SERIES

THE AMERICAN EAGLE

THE AMERICAN MUSTANG

THE NORTH AMERICAN WOLF

THE NORTH AMERICAN BIGHORN SHEEP

THE AMERICAN ALLIGATOR

THE AMERICAN PRAIRIE CHICKEN

THE BALANCE OF NATURE SERIES

A DAY AND A NIGHT IN A FOREST

A DAY AND A NIGHT IN THE ARCTIC

Holiday House

GARDEN SPIDER

HONEYBEE

FIDDLER CRAB

GRAY SQUIRREL

Houghton Mifflin

THE FIREHOUSE MYSTERY

THE TUGBOAT MYSTERY

THE CITY SCIENCE SERIES

SECRET NEIGHBORS:

Wildlife in a City Lot

By MARY ADRIAN

Illustrated by Jean Zallinger

HASTINGS HOUSE • PUBLISHERS
New York

Published simultaneously in Canada by
Saunders, of Toronto, Ltd., Don Mills, Ontario

ISBN: 8038-6708-5

Library of Congress Catalog Card Number: 79-170628
Printed in the United States of America

CONTENTS

THE FIELD MOUSE

AN APRIL breeze fanned the leaves of an ailanthus tree. It was growing alongside a wooden fence that partly edged a vacant city lot. The wind set sail to the paper that littered the ground and ruffled the brown fur of a field mouse.

She was a pretty little animal with bright eyes and long whiskers that quivered in the cool morning air.

Inside her burrow under a rock was her family — seven little mice, less than a week old. The mother had just finished nursing them and felt she needed some food herself.

Field Mouse looked carefully about for danger. She took in every sight and sound since she had many enemies, especially an alley cat that was always on the prowl for mice.

Feeling that the coast was clear, Field Mouse scampered along a trail through weeds, grass and rubble. The path had been made by her and other field mice living in the city lot. She scurried between broken glass and empty tin cans. Overhead a flock of pigeons had been circling round and round. Two dropped from the formation and began feeding on garbage that someone had thrown in the foundation of a torn-down apartment house.

Field Mouse skirted the foundation and came face to face with a starling. Starling's feathers were edged in brown and his breast was speckled with white dots. But his plumage was dirty from the city smoke. The small bird was busy eating breadcrumbs that an old lady had left on a pie pan.

Starling looked up, stared at Field Mouse for a few seconds, and then continued with his breakfast.

Field Mouse went on through tangled grass and litter. Finally, she came to her favorite eat-

ing place — a patch of red clover that had bloomed last year but had many seeds left. New clover shoots were coming up, too.

Field Mouse ate and ate until she was very full. She looked around again for danger, sniffed the air and twitched her whiskers. Everything seemed safe. So she started on the return trip to her nest. Just as she was nearing the end of her trail, she had the scare of her life.

The swishing sound of wings filled the air. A sparrow hawk was out hunting for food and had seen Field Mouse.

9

Quick as a flash Field Mouse darted through an opening in an empty can. It was just big enough for her to get through.

Sparrow Hawk dropped low. With an angry cry, he flew upward.

Field Mouse crawled way back inside the can. Her heart beat wildly because she knew that Sparrow Hawk was a good hunter and was not going to give up easily.

A few seconds later Sparrow Hawk landed on the ground alongside the can. He stuck his bill inside the opening.

Field Mouse was terrified. She held still, so still that not even a whisker moved.

Sparrow Hawk was determined to get his prey. He pecked at the can with his bill, making a clinking sound.

Field Mouse did not budge. She stayed at the
far end of the can, huddled into a ball.

It was not long before she saw two dark eyes
peer inside the can. The next thing she knew she
turned upside down and then rightside up.

Sparrow Hawk had turned over the can several times with his bill. Then, with a disgusted cry, he gave up the hunt and flew away.

Field Mouse waited until she felt all danger was past. She poked her head outside. She looked around and listened for the swish of wings, but all she heard was the steady drone of city traffic. So she came all the way outside. Then she ran back to her nest where she found her babies fast asleep, snuggled against each other.

Field Mouse lay down beside them, but she trembled with fright. Escaping from a hunter like Sparrow Hawk had been a terrifying experience. The next time she went on an outing for food, she would be more alert for enemies.

SITTING ON EGGS

As THE day wore on the weather grew warmer. A queen bumblebee buzzed on a dandelion growing alongside the fence. She had awakened a few days ago from her winter's sleep in a crack in the ground under some rubble.

Now Queen Bumblebee sipped the nectar in the dandelion, went to another dandelion, and drank more sweet liquid. Then she circled low above a tuft of crab grass near the fence and a second later disappeared into a shallow hole in the ground. This was her nest.

Queen Bumblebee was getting ready to lay her eggs. At the entrance to her nest she paused and squeezed wax from her body to make a tiny

honey pot. She filled the pot with a mixture of nectar and pollen that she had gathered from dandelions so that she would have food.

Then she made some wax cups and spread a

layer of pollen in each one so that when the eggs hatched, her off-spring would have food too. After that Queen Bumblebee laid eight eggs. She sat on them the way birds sit on their eggs.

Outside Queen Bumblebee's nest, other wild creatures were stirring after their winter's sleep. A woolly bear caterpillar crawled out from under a loose board where she had spent the winter curled up in a tight ball. Her tiny head was shiny black, and her body was striped in reddish-brown and black. She could not see with her small eyes, so she used her feelers, reaching in every direction until she felt a weed stalk. She climbed up it and ate some leaves. Then she spun a cocoon around herself.

On another weed stalk baby spiders were about to leave their small pear-shaped nest. One spider cut a tiny hole in the top and squeezed through the opening. The others followed and soon the weed stalk was covered with many tiny spiders. They crawled down to the ground and explored the grass littered with rubble.

In a few days the tiny spiders were ready to see the world. They crawled up weed stalks and spun out lines of silk. A strong breeze tossed their lines back and forth. The spiders held on tightly. Soon their lines were blown away, and the tiny spiders sailed into the air. They sailed so high that soon they were above tall buildings. On and on the wind carried them over fields, towns and other cities. They would land in many different places.

One spider who had left a nest in a meadow miles away, landed in the city lot. Immediately she started spinning a web to catch food. She spun lines to a plantain, a weed with tall spikes of tiny flowers. Then she spun spiral threads of silk, going round and round from the center to the edge of the web. After that she spun sticky spiral lines to trap her prey and she cut away the old spiral lines.

Spider's web was finished now. It was a small web since she was very young, but it would serve its purpose. She oiled herself so that she could

17

hurry over the sticky lines in case an insect fell
into her trap.

Near Spider's web tiny grasshoppers had
freed themselves from their egg shells in the
ground. They pushed upward through the soil
— pale wingless creatures with huge heads and

cellophane coverings that were too large for them. Each grasshopper soon got rid of its baggy skin, took a few steps, and jumped.

One little grasshopper tipped over at the end of her leap. She picked herself up quickly and crawled up the stem of a plant. She held the edge of a leaf between her front feet. She bit a hole in it and had her first meal.

Grasshopper's brother did not fare as well. He crawled up a stem of the plantain and stumbled into Spider's web. He kicked and kicked, trying to free himself from the sticky lines.

It was no use. Spider ran across her web. She pounced upon the tiny grasshopper, killed him and sucked the juices from his body. After mending the broken strands in her web, she waited for more prey to come by.

THE SINGING CATS

SPRING was now in full bloom. Clusters of green flowers hung like plumes from the ailanthus tree.

A pair of pigeons were feeding their young on a window ledge of a brownstone house on the corner of the lot. A woman had put out some bread crumbs for them. A sparrow and his mate were also gathering food for their family. They picked up caterpillars, plant lice, and other insects to bring back to the nest.

It was a pleasant day. A brightly-painted ice cream truck stopped by the corner. The ice cream man rang his bell and was immediately surrounded by a large group of impatient people.

Children rode their bicycles on the sidewalk to avoid the buses and cars in the street. Some boys were playing catch in the lot, laughing and yelling at each other. As it grew later, one by one the children left for home, and the lot was quiet again.

Gradually darkness descended upon the city lot broken by shafts of light from illuminated windows of an apartment house.

Near an old deserted warehouse at one end of the lot was an alley where a cat was sleeping inside a wooden crate. He got up, stretched, and yawned. He had scraggly yellow fur and a body as thin as a reed. Alley Cat's life was not an easy one since his food was mainly scraps of garbage and mice and rats he could catch.

Quietly Alley Cat walked away from the warehouse, stopped, and looked around. He was checking to see if a big dog was prowling nearby. He often visited the lot, so Alley Cat always was on guard.

Since there was no sign of the dog, Alley Cat ambled over to the ailanthus tree. He climbed up the trunk to a sturdy branch and looked down from his perch. Suddenly he saw something move — something with shiny black fur. It was a female house cat. With her fluffy tail out straight she sauntered over to a garbage can.

Alley Cat carefully started down the tree. At the last few feet he leaped to the ground. Then staying a short distance from the female cat, he began to yowl. This was his song. The female listened with twitching whiskers.

Before long Alley Cat was joined by another male cat and together they serenaded the female.

Once more she listened attentively and then moved her tail back and forth.

After a while Alley Cat and his rival stopped singing. They started to fight to win the female. Shrieking and howling, they rolled over each other on the ground. They pulled out wads of fur with their hind claws. Taking a breathing spell, they got up and backed away from each other. They came together again. This time Alley Cat bit of a small part of his rival's ear.

Screaming, the male cat got up and ran away.

Alley Cat waited until he was out of sight. Then he and the female wandered off together down the alley.

Later that night there was another loud noise. A speeding car had narrowly missed the big dog. He jumped to the sidewalk and crashed into a garbage can. Potato peelings, coffee grinds, egg shells, and empty containers lay on the ground.

The dog sniffed at the spilled garbage. He

found nothing he liked so he poked his head into the can and backed out with a large bone. With a wag of his tail he trotted off with it.

A few moments later six roaches squeezed out of their hiding place in the apartment house basement. They were small dark insects with long feelers and six legs. The roaches waved their feelers in the darkness and caught the smell of garbage. They could not see very well so they flicked their feelers some more to lead them to the food.

Soon the roaches were crawling over the scraps of garbage on the ground. They were so busy eating that at first they did not notice four brown rats who had just arrived. They had sneaked out of a hole in the old warehouse and twitched their noses in the darkness, seeking out every odor. Being scavengers like the roaches, the rats immediately began eating some potato peels. The roaches kept out of their way.

A short while later Alley Cat came back to the weed lot to see if he could find a garbage can that was not tightly closed. To his surprise he not only smelled garbage but also rats. Without making a sound Alley Cat moved closer to his prey. The rats were busy at their feast. He crouched, ready to spring.

Just then one rat caught the scent of Alley Cat. Instantly he started running to the old warehouse. The other rats dashed after him.

Alley Cat followed, his legs moving swiftly.

In went one rat through the small hole in the wall of the warehouse. Next came the other two rats. The last rat was a second too late. Alley Cat pounced on him and killed him.

After he had eaten the dead rat, he cleaned his whiskers and returned to the garbage can. The roaches were no longer there. They had taken to cover because light had flooded the garbage can from an apartment house window.

Alley Cat looked over the contents of the garbage can. His whiskers twitched excitedly. There was a broken dish with some tuna on it. Alley Cat licked the plate clean. After that he curled up in his wooden crate in the alley and dropped off to sleep.

THE FIDDLER

SPRING was replaced by the warm days of summer. The faded flowers on the ailanthus tree were dropping their petals. The yellowish-green leaves that hung from the ends of the branches were covered with city soot.

One moonlit night Field Mouse decided to go on an outing for food. She was raising her third family since that day she had fled into an empty can to escape from Sparrow Hawk. Some of her young had died of disease and others had been eaten by Sparrow Hawk and Alley Cat. Field Mouse had been fortunate to escape from her enemies.

Now she pitter-pattered along a trail in the

grass. She stopped and sniffed at an old shoe. A beetle crawled out of it and looked at her with inquisitive eyes, then turned and shot back into its hiding place.

Field Mouse went on, her bright eyes taking in everything around her. She saw a yellowish-brown moth with dark spots alight on a plant. It was an Isabella tiger moth that had come out of the cocoon made by a woolly-bear caterpillar in the spring.

Field Mouse was not interested in the Isabella tiger moth. She was anxious to find food. She stopped and ate some seeds and the roots of grasses. Then she sniffed the air vigorously for a danger signal. All that came to her were the usual city sounds. Field Mouse ate some more seeds and then hurried back to nurse her babies, not yet a day old.

As she approached her nest, she passed a cricket chirping a song. He was in front of his short burrow that went under a pile of bricks near the fence.

Cricket was a tiny coal-black creature. Like his cousin, Grasshopper, he had hatched from an egg in the ground in late spring. He had shed his skin several times and was now a full grown cricket with wings.

After a while Cricket stopped making music and began eating some plants. His jaws moved sideways as he chewed the leaves. When he felt full, he polished the sides of his body with his hind legs. He also cleaned his feelers. Then Cricket went by Grasshopper who was sleeping on a weed stalk and tickled him with his feelers.

Instantly Grasshopper awoke and jumped to the next weed stalk.

Cricket would have teased him some more, but just then he saw another cricket sitting in front of his burrow. Cricket rushed at the intruder. He kicked him with his front legs.

The stranger fought back. He struck out and kicked hard with his legs.

Cricket jumped to one side. He rushed at the intruder again. They came together head-on, but Cricket was stronger. He pushed his opponent backward. He lashed out with his legs and kicked him very hard.

The stranger decided he had had enough. He moved away.

Cricket went and sat in front of his burrow.

A short while later he raised his wings and, scraping one across the edge of the other, played music the way a person plays a violin. Cricket was fiddling for a mate.

It was not long before a female heard Cricket's music. Like him she had eardrums, one on each side of her front legs, but she could not chirp because her wings were not built for playing music.

She listened to the chirping sound Cricket made. Soon she moved in his direction.

Cricket saw her coming. He welcomed her with more music. She stopped and allowed him to stroke her feelers. Then they went off together.

HONEYDEW

HOT SUMMER days arrived. Flies buzzed around soda bottles, old candy and ice cream wrappers which had been tossed in the city lot.

In the street, a team of workmen were fixing a broken water main. The loud noise of their machines clattered on and on. The noise frightened away the pigeons who had been roosting on the apartment house ledge. The lady kept leaving breadcrumbs by the window, but the birds didn't come back.

In the lot below, an ant crawled out of his nest, a hole in the ground under an old tire. He looked around. Then he zigzagged past some broken glass and hurried by clumps of grass. When he came to an old rubber ball he stopped and smelled it with his feelers. Remembering the ball as a signpost, he continued on his way.

Finally Ant saw a large caterpiller at the foot of the ailanthus tree. Ant came up and smelled the creature with his feelers. It was dead. He tugged at it, but it was too big for him to haul to the nest. So Ant started back the way he had come, leaving a trail of liquid on the ground. Ant was making a trail scent for other ants in his colony.

No sooner had Ant arrived at the nest than he and several workers followed his trail back to the dead caterpillar. They took turns pulling the creature to the nest.

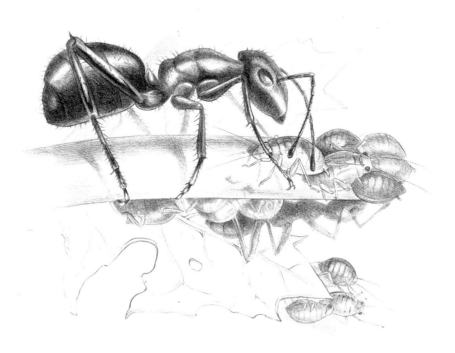

After that Ant continued to scout for more food. This time he went to a patch of dandelions. On the stems were many tiny pale green insects called aphids. They had fat bodies, long feelers, round eyes, and mouths shaped with sucking tubes.

The aphids were busy sucking juices from the dandelions. But the tiny insects also gave honeydew, a sweet liquid which ants like to eat.

Ant started back to his colony, leaving another trail scent as he scurried along.

He brought back many workers that gathered at the dandelions. They climbed up the stems and began stroking the sides and backs of the aphids with their feelers.

In return for the stroking the insects poured the sweet honeydew out from the tips of their bodies.

Ant quickly lapped up the liquid, stroked another aphid and had some more honeydew. He kept doing this until he was so full he could not lick up another drop.

But Ant did not leave the dandelions. Instead, he stayed there with the other workers, and guarded the aphids from enemies.

Toward mid-afternoon heavy grey clouds gathered in the sky. Before long big raindrops began to fall. One hit Ant on the head, another on his back.

Ant did not like rain, and he did not like to get wet. Helter-skelter, Ant and the other workers hurried back to their nest under the old tire. They huddled together in their dark underground cavern to wait out the storm.

Soon streaks of lightning flashed across the sky and thunder sounded like the beating of many drums. Now the rain came down in torrents. The workmen ran to their trucks for cover.

The rain drenched the lot, soaking through old newspapers which the wind scattered every-where.

Cricket jumped several times and took refuge in his burrow under the pile of bricks.

The aphids stayed where they were, clinging to the dandelion stems.

Grasshopper and other insects sought the overhanging leaves of plants and hid under them.

Even Starling flew to a protected ledge of the apartment house to get out of the rain.

For a good half hour the storm raged. Then it passed as suddenly as it came, and gradually the wild creatures came out of hiding. Ant decided to go back to the dandelions. The other workers followed, one in back of the other.

But when they reached their destination, they found tiny round orange-red beetles had arrived before them. They were ladybugs and they were eating the aphids.

Ant and the workers rushed up the dandelion stems. They attacked the ladybugs with their pincers.

The ladybugs quickly flew away — all except one. She stayed on the dandelion and ate another aphid.

Ant grabbed Ladybug by the leg. She pulled away and dropped to the ground. She lay there on her back with her feet curled up.

Ant hurried down the dandelion stem. Ladybug looked dead and Ant did not know that she was only pretending. So he went back up the dandelion and stroked an aphid.

A few moments later Ant saw Ladybug on another dandelion eating an aphid. This time he really chased Ladybug away. Then he went after another feast of honeydew.

THE TRAP-LINE

A MOSQUITO alighted on the edge of an upright can in the city lot. It was a soup can filled with rainwater from the storm.

Mosquito looked and carefully laid about a hundred eggs in the water.

In a few days the eggs hatched and larvae came out. They looked nothing like their mother. Tiny and wiggly, they lived beneath the surface of the water. After about a week the larvae changed into pupae. Inside their skins, the pupae slowly changed form. Finally their change was complete. They split their old skins and took to the air as adult mosquitoes.

Around the lot they flew. The females made a

humming sound and hunted for animal blood. The males made a much quieter hum and sucked the juices from the stems of plants.

One male mosquito landed on top of a FOR SALE sign in front of the lot and began cleaning himself. He did not notice that Spider had spun a web between the sign and a ragweed plant growing next to it. The web was larger than the one she had made in the spring, because Spider was now full grown.

As was her custom Spider lay waiting for prey to stumble into her trap. But she was nowhere in sight. She was sitting under some ragweed leaves with a silk line running from her hiding place to her web. It was her trap-line.

Soon the male mosquito left his perch and flew to the stem of a cocklebur growing nearby. He sucked juice from it and then darted to the ragweed by the FOR SALE sign. The mosquito could hear well with his feathery feelers, but only familiar noises came to him — car horns honking, the din of workmen — so he continued sipping ragweed juice undisturbed. He climbed farther up the plant and drank more juice. He

came closer and closer to Spider's web, but all
he saw were a lot of silk lines.

Then the mosquito stepped into the trap. He
shook the web, struggling to get free from the
sticky lines.

Immediately Spider's trap-line wiggled. It sig-
nalled to her that something was caught in her
web.

Spider ran along her trap-line, which acted as a bridge. She rushed into her web and seized the helpless mosquito. She bit him and killed him.

After Spider had eaten him, she mended her broken silk lines and went back to her hiding place to wait for a signal that more prey had fallen into her web.

THE OLD SHOE

AUTUMN HAD come to the city lot. Leaves from the ailanthus tree twirled through the air and fell silently to the ground.

It was a quiet time. The workmen had finished their job and were gone. The children had returned to school.

The only noise came from the wind. It blew the leaves over plants that had turned brown. The cold breeze also swept some leaves against the fence where a few dandelions still bloomed.

Field Mouse sniffed the cool morning air. It was time for her to store food for the coming winter and to find a place for a winter nest. She scouted around and finally selected a clump of

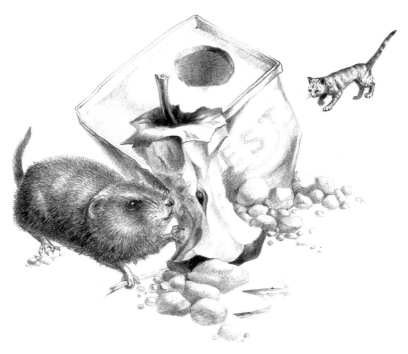

weeds where she wove a nest of string, grasses,
and bits of ribbon. Then she went and dug up
dandelion roots and put them in a hole under an
old stump. After that she set out on another trip
to bring more food back to her underground
storeroom.

When Field Mouse began her journey she did
not know that Alley Cat was on the prowl for
prey. He had caught several young mice during
the summer, but as yet he had not been able to

get near Field Mouse because she was so swift.

This morning Alley Cat had caught Field Mouse's scent on one of her hidden trails. The weeds swayed back and forth as Alley Cat slinked along quietly — his one thought being to sneak up and pounce upon Field Mouse.

It was not long before he saw his prey sniffing around an old apple core. Alley Cat's bright eyes glistened with hunger. He crouched low. He took a few steps toward Field Mouse.

Just then Field Mouse looked up. She twitched her whiskers because the scent of Alley Cat filled the air.

Nervously, Field Mouse looked this way and that way, but she didn't see Alley Cat hiding in the tall weeds.

Field Mouse was not taking any chances, and she must act quickly since the scent was very strong now. Which way should she go?

Field Mouse dashed to the left.

Quick as a flash Alley Cat sprang forward. He missed grabbing Field Mouse by a few inches.

Terrified, Field Mouse darted through the weeds. She was not on one of her secret trails, so

the territory was unfamiliar, but her bright eyes
soon spotted an old tire. She circled it. She
stopped and looked around. Alley Cat was nowhere in sight, and no danger scent came back
to her. Field Mouse carefully started toward her
nest, taking the shortest route.

No sooner had she come near her nest than

she saw a clump of weeds move. The next thing she knew a bundle of yellow fur came into view. Alley Cat was waiting for her.

With pounding heart Field Mouse turned and headed for the old shoe near her nest. She shot inside like a flying bullet.

The beetle did not like to see Field Mouse in his hiding place, but there was nothing he could do about it.

Field Mouse curled up at the far end of the shoe and waited, every nerve tense, every whisker quivering.

Minutes went by. Alley Cat, still hiding in the weeds, stayed close to Field Mouse's nest.

After a while Alley Cat grew impatient and was just about to leave when he saw another field mouse come and sniff at the weeds.

Alley Cat quietly sneaked up behind the mouse, pounced on him, and killed him.

As he slinked off with his prey dangling from his mouth, Field Mouse peeked out of the old shoe. She saw Alley Cat. She ducked back into her hiding place, waited until the coast was clear, then scooted into her nest and disappeared.

GETTING READY
FOR WINTER

THE NEXT morning Spider crawled up the For Sale sign. She had mated in late summer and was about to lay her eggs. She spun an egg case and attached it to the bottom edge of the sign. She laid about five hundred eggs in it, and spun more silk around the case until it looked like a pear-shaped nest.

Spider's work was finished. In a few days her life would end, but until that time she would stay and guard her eggs.

Nearby, Cricket was playing music very quietly. Cricket fiddled very little now because of the frosty nights and the cool days. His mate was busy laying their eggs. She pierced the soil with her oviposter that looked like a long tail. She laid her eggs, one by one, in the ground near the fence. After that, the female cricket died.

In a little while Cricket played his last song, and his life also came to an end.

Grasshopper clung to a weed stalk. He, too, would soon leave this world. He watched his mate drill tiny holes in the ground at the end of the lot. She laid her eggs in them. Then she rested for the last time.

Ant was busy storing away food for next spring. He dragged a small beetle into his underground nest under the old tire. He came outside and was joined by other worker ants in his colony. After they had filled their storeroom, the ants clustered together in their nest and went to sleep.

Ladybug was ready for her winter sleep, too. It was not long before she and several other ladybug beetles tucked themselves away in cracks in the wall of the brownstone house.

A reddish-brown and black woolly bear caterpillar was also looking for a place to hibernate.

He was the offspring of the tiger moth who had laid her eggs in the lot during the summer.

Woolly Bear Caterpillar moved slowly past a patch of crab grass growing near a pile of bricks. He stopped and examined the grass, but it would not make a good hibernating place. So Woolly Bear crawled on at the same slow pace.

As he came near the fence, Starling landed on the ground alongside him. Feeling that Woolly Bear would make a good meal, the bird flicked his tail with excitement.

Immediately Woolly Bear curled into a tight little ball as if he were dead.

Starling walked around Woolly Bear and studied him closely.

Woolly Bear did not move.

Gingerly, Starling poked him with his bill then quickly drew away. He did not like the feel of Woolly Bear's hair. Deciding he could catch a more appetizing meal, Starling lifted his wings and flew away.

Woolly Bear slowly uncurled himself. He moved along until he came to a trash pile by the old warehouse. Old hair curlers and three paper cups had been thrown on a heap of rags, empty cartons, old magazines, and bottles. Here was a good place for Woolly Bear to spend his long winter's sleep.

As he crawled under the rubbish heap, a young queen bumblebee began looking for winter quarters in the city lot. She was all alone since the old queen bee and her entire colony died when the cold weather began.

Now Bumblebee circled a small hole in the

ground. She peered inside and then disappeared down its mouth.

A second later Bumblebee came flying out. Close behind her was the owner of the hole, a large black spider.

Bumblebee was not discouraged. She alighted on a late-blooming dandelion, sipped some nectar, and then continued looking for a winter home.

She was not aware that a large robber fly was watching, waiting for the right moment to attack her with the sharp dagger in his beak. As he rested on a plant, he saw Bumblebee crawling along the ground near the fence. Here was his chance.

Just as the robber fly took off, Bumblebee turned around and spotted her enemy.

Immediately Bumblebee flew up. They met head-on in the air. They grabbed hold of each other and fell to the ground. They rolled over.

The robber fly tried to bite Bumblebee with his beak, but she was too quick for him. She jabbed her powerful stinger into him and killed him.

After that Bumblebee continued searching for a winter home. She finally found a snug place under the trash pile where Woolly Bear was hibernating. Bumblebee made herself comfortable. Then she too dropped off into a deep sleep.

THE WHITE BLANKET

WINTER HAD come to the city lot. As the days passed, the north wind grew stronger and colder, tossing dead weed stalks to and fro, and sent litter flying.

Underground the grasshopper and cricket eggs were snug and warm because soil holds heat in winter.

The eggs in the pear-shaped nest that Spider had made on the For Sale sign were also cozy and protected. Only some of the eggs had already hatched and tiny baby spiders pushed and bumped into one another. Some were hungry. The stronger ones ate the weaker ones.

Field Mouse went by the spider's nest, but

showed no interest. She was concerned about a mouse who had come into the city lot. He was a stranger, and Field Mouse did not like strangers. She did not mind mice who lived in the lot. But an intruder was different.

This morning Field Mouse saw the stranger again near her nest in the clump of weeds. Clicking her teeth in rage, she darted up to the intruder. She kicked him with her front feet.

The stranger fought back. He struck out with his front feet, his claws slashing through Field Mouse's fur and skin.

Field Mouse was enraged. She bit the stranger with her sharp teeth right on the nose.

Squeaking with pain the intruder backed away. Realizing he was the loser, he turned and left.

Field Mouse waited until he was out of sight. Then she dashed into her nest.

Later that day snow flurries filled the air. Large flakes soon danced their way to the ground, and before long the city lot was covered with a white blanket.

Field Mouse did not mind. She was safe in her snow-covered nest. She had food, too, stored away in her storeroom under the old stump.

All night the snow fell silently. By morning it had stopped and a weak sun shone in the sky.

Field Mouse began digging a tunnel under the snow. Her tunnels were important because they protected her from Alley Cat and the sharp eyes of Sparrow Hawk. Soon she found the top of a buried weed with fat seeds attached to it. Field Mouse had a good breakfast. Later, when she was hungry again, she tunneled to her underground storeroom for more food.

By afternoon the weather became warmer and melting snow dripped from the branches of the

ailanthus tree. Puddles formed here and there, edged with snow that was already dirty from city smoke.

The rest of the winter brought many more cold days but not much snow. Sparrows and starlings lived on weed seeds and food scraps put out for them by neighbors.

Alley Cat rummaged through garbage cans that the big dog knocked over. The rats ate what was left by Alley Cat. And the roaches stayed in warm places because they did not like the cold weather.

Finally it was spring and the city lot became alive with activity.

Field Mouse had lived longer than most mice. She was very old now, but still scurried as quickly as ever along hidden trails through the grass and litter.

Bumblebee left her hiding place under the trash pile and looked for a hole to lay her eggs.

Woolly Bear uncurled himself and crawled out from under the same trash heap. He went and nipped off bits of leaves and ate them. Then he spun a cocoon on the underside of a loose board.

Baby spiders deserted their nest on the FOR SALE sign and floated away on their silk lines.

Ant awoke with the others in his colony in their underground nest under the old tire. They ate the food in their storeroom and then came outside.

Ladybug left the crack in the brick wall and flew about, looking for aphids on plants.

Eggs hatched in the ground and baby grasshoppers and crickets came out and saw the world in a city lot for the first time.

BIBLIOGRAPHY

Allen, Gertrude: *Everyday Insects*, Boston, Houghton Mifflin Co., 1963.

Blough, Glenn O.: *Discovering Insects*, New York, McGraw-Hill Book Co., 1967.

Bronson, Wilfred S.: *The Grasshopper Book*, New York, Harcourt, Brace & World, Inc., 1943.

Buck, Margaret Waring: *Where They Go In Winter*, New York, Nashville, Abingdon Press, 1968.

Cahalane, Victor H.: *Mammals of North America*, New York, Macmillan Co., 1947.

Cohen, Daniel: *Animals Of The City*, New York, McGraw-Hill Book Co., 1969.

Earle, Olive L.: *Crickets*, New York, William E. Morrow & Co., 1956.

National Audubon Society: *The Audubon Nature Encyclopedia*, Philadelphia-New York, Curtis Pub. Co., 1964.

National Geographic Society: *Wild Animals of North America*, Washington, D.C., National Geographic Society, 1960.

Schneider, Gerald: *Nature In The City*, Ranger Rick Magazine, April 1970, Washington, D.C., National Wildlife Federation, Inc.

Stefferud, Alfred: *Birds In Our Lives*, Washington, D.C., The U.S. Dept. of the Interior, Bureau of Sport Fisheries and Wildlife, 1966.

Teale, Edwin Way: *Where Do Insects Go In Winter?* Natural History Magazine, January 1943, New York, The American Museum of Natural History. *Grassroot Jungles*, New York, Dodd, Mead & Co., 1937.

The American Museum of Natural History: *The Illustrated Encyclopedia of Animal Life*, New York, Greystone Press, 1961.

62

INDEX

pupae (mosquito), 41

ragweed, 42
rats, 26-27, 59
roaches, 26-28, 59
robber fly, 54

sparrow, 21, 59

sparrowhawk, 9-11, 29, 58
spiders, 15, 17-18, 20, 42-44, 50,
    54, 56, 60
  eggs, 50, 56
spiderweb, 17, 20, 42-44
starling, 8, 39, 52-53, 59

wooly bear, *see* caterpillar